Advance Praise

"I loved Seth Brady Tucker's first book, *Mormon Boy*, and I love this one more. Whether he is speaking of (as) Wile E. Coyote metaphorically, or speaking as a man who jumped out of airplanes (not for fun) and fired and was fired upon, or when he is speaking his remarkable love poems, you know you are hearing (I'm purposefully using 'speaking' and 'hearing' instead of writing and reading) something authentic, and true."

 —Thomas Lux, author of *God Particles* and *Split Horizon*

"The poems in Seth Brady Tucker's *We Deserve The Gods We Ask For* are acrobatic and epic and make me happy that poetry is still a place where we can re-envision the old questions about life and the spirit. In the book, I hear echoes of our great American masters, like Ashbery, Hemingway, Plath, Merwin, and Stein, infused in a new voice with the rhetorical bravado of a 100 swallows swarming the forest, 1000 preachers booming the word of the soul, and 10,000 conductors of a never-ending symphony of being that extends from this world into the next. Bravo to this poet, who tells us so nonchalantly it is: 'God here. As in *big G* God. As in, listen up.' Listen up. Read this book."

 —Dorothea Lasky, author of *ROME*

"Through these poems echo 'the vibrations/of bare feet on hollow concrete... /at first like children at play, /and then like children at war, /and then feet shuffling in blood.' Seth Brady Tucker writes of cartoon heroes, soldiers, lost brothers, new lovers, and undying ghosts with humor, pathos, wit, and remorse. The poems in *We Deserve the Gods We Ask For* want to break your heart. If you let them, they will."

—Camille T. Dungy, author of *Smith Blue*

"Pain of dreaming over din of cartoons with pharmaceutical advertisements has answers in the courage Seth Brady Tucker brings to poetry. We're leaning on the doorjamb of his experience, a soldier letting air back into his lungs, and our lungs, one line at a time. 'Spirit am listens to god noise. Spirit am translate. Spirit am move, live, work, for god noise.' A poet who listens for the rest of us to the pulse that could be our blood, could be a man falling from the sky, could be love with a pen and a helmet. This book is nothing less than amazing!"

—CAConrad, author of *ECODEVIANCE*

"Gritty and unflinching, the poems in Seth B. Tucker's *We Deserve the Gods We Ask For* confront the contested territory between resignation and resilience in a world where suffering is imminent. From paratroopers to Popeye, Tucker gives us hardened vantage points that survey the 'losses only faith can redeem.' This is sinewy writing at its most sturdy and tenacious. His—tangle of silk and muscle—is sure to stagger and transfix."

—Lisa Graley, judge and author of *Box of Blue Horses*

For Benjamin— Heres to the day I am able to sign your book!

We Deserve The Gods We Ask For

Seth Brady Tucker

Winner of the Gival Press Poetry Award

Gival Press

Arlington, Virginia

Seaside 5/17/17

Published by Gival Press, an imprint of Gival Press, LLC.
For information please write:
Gival Press, LLC
P. O. Box 3812
Arlington, VA 22203
www.givalpress.com

First edition
ISBN: 978-1-928589-93-8
eISBN: 978-1-928589-94-5
Library of Congress Control Number: 2014947587

Cover Art: *Filling Little Thoughts With Little Ears*.
Painting by Joe Sorren. All Rights Reserved.
www.joesorren.com

Photo of Seth Brady Tucker by Rob Clement.
Book Design by Ken Schellenberg.

Table of Contents

III. Death is a Prayer

Acknowledgments

Grateful acknowledgement and my deepest thanks is due to the editors of the following literary magazines and/or online publications where these poems appeared, sometimes in slightly different form.

Apalachee Review: "Sandman."
Asheville Poetry Review: "Supply Tent."
Chattahoochee Review: "His Pomeranian" and "Popeye, Off Camera."
Chautauqua: "Spam."
The Connecticut Review: "Aqua Man."
Epiphany: "Cold Is Cold Everywhere."
Harpur Palate: "Godot's Underpants" and "Bayou."
Main Street Rag: "The Contract" (published as "The Contract I Signed").
Mountain Gazette: "Hot Tarmac" and "Two Long Years."
Poetry Northwest: "Spirit Listens to God" (published as "Spirit Speaks") and "Stovepipe."
River Styx: "Watermelon Truck Near Araby, Georgia."
Rosebud: "Zoloft."
Southern Humanities Review: "Memphis."
storySouth: "Major Tom to Ground Control."
Water~Stone Review: "Wile E. Coyote."

I am grateful to the following early readers, without whom I would have simply kept beating my face against the keyboard: John Cady, David Kirby, Jane Springer, and Ellen Bryant Voigt.

I am also deeply indebted to Matt Bondurant, Camille T. Dungy, Kava Felmlee, Andrew McFadyen-Ketchum, Toni Lefton, Nils Michals, and Olivia Tucker, who gave me the deep editing advice that turned this manuscript from an "also ran" to a winner to a book.

Of course, Robert Giron at *Gival Press* has been a peach, and I can't leave out *Elixir Press* and Dana Curtis, who I will always feel "discovered me" and launched my career as a real poet (or at least, made me feel like one).

A sincere thank you to Joe Sorren for his wonderful artwork.

Endless thanks to my literary and scholarly gods, who heard me when
I prayed for things I may not have deserved: my agent, Alex Glass,
and Julianna Baggott, Reginald Dwayne Betts, CA Conrad, Jonathan
D'Avignon, David J. Daniels, Shann Ray Ferch, Barbara Hamby, Dorothea
Lasky, Thomas Lux, David Rothman, Steven Schwartz, Luis Alberto
Urrea, Mark Winegardner, Kathryn Winograd, and Jake Adam York. I am
indebted to you all for kindnesses big and small.

Thank you Andrea and Mike and everyone at the Lighthouse Writers'
Workshop, for giving me a community to cherish, and students to serve; and
to the University of Colorado at Boulder (Program for Writing and Rhetoric
and the English Department) and the Colorado School of Mines.

Thanks to the Tennessee Williams endowment and all the fine folks at the
Sewanee Writers' Conference, as well as Carol Houck Smith endowment
and everyone at Bread Loaf Writers' Conference for their faith in my work.

This book would not exist without the love and support and belief and trust
of Olivia Tucker, who was sent by the universe to save me.

Finally, thank you dear friends and family—you are all the gods I have ever
needed.

mortifera desupra

In the Beginning

Because it cannot begin
in any other way, it begins
in the beginning with there was dust,
and from the dust there was sky and because there was dust
and sky there was wind and the wind was ochre and rust
with the dust and into the wind and the dust
was a child of gardens borne, and a child of forest, and then a child or sea,
and because there was already wind and dust, and let's face it,
there were rocks and boulders and terrible cliff faces
and valleys and bones of mountains——all there for the wind
to gnaw upon and devour and shit out
until it was totally fucked up and dry and barren,
and into this place, the robotic children of man, their telos
to dig and rumble and taste with tongues lolling
from vacuum sealed orifices, fingers angled and bifurcated, digging
claws square-cornered, hearts like dragonflies nano-carved
from carbon bocce balls, linear and straight as rulers
in this new world suffuse only
with red craggy canals
and righteous natural curves.

"I'm not normally a praying man, but if you're
up there, please save me, Superman!"
—— Homer Simpson

"I'm cold," Snowden said again in a frail, childlike voice. "I'm cold."
"There, there," Yossarian said, because he did not
know what else to say. "There, there."
—— Joseph Heller, *Catch-22*

I. Bing Bang Biff Pow

Beautiful Boys in Brodie Helmets

We hole up until shelling is over, ducked
in cover, held by frozen earth, beneath
rail ties, and even desperately under shovels.

For some, the hope like an umbrella
of prayer, a cry for protection under
the thin blade of an entrenching tool.

And some of us even make
it home, to the pastoral noise
of Shropshire or the cobbled industry

of London, and we wash dishes
in copper basins absently, our family
simply background noise to our thoughts:

remember the stink of the dead mule,
too much to bear until we were all
surrounded by the fetal dead, their hands

always closed in loose fists, tucked
to their chests like they held the reins
to a plow-horse, some stopped even as they

made ready to warm their icy pink hands with
the hot exhalation of their very last breath.

Wile E. Coyote

It began with Percocet, Valium, and Vicodin,
as it so often does, after so many gruesome
falls from terrific heights, after all the bone

grinding dust clouds of Smash! Bam! Crunch!
So many locomotives bearing heavy freight
out of painted-on tunnels, a trick, certainly,

of corporate America, of sponsors like Acme,
Ford, or Calgon and the ancient Chinese betrayal
of clean clothes. But these sound like excuses

now, because I was the contracted stuntman,
the demolition expert, the adrenaline junkie,
then a real junkie, white horse the only thing left

to ride. And you were taking your thick runner's
legs to Acme University anyway, full ride, slumming
with me even though I was famous, and what happens

then is what always happens—city girl dumps
country boy. It was too much, I guess; us fucking
on the first night, our fire stoked with alcohol, ludes,

and ecstasy. Then the horror of the morning after,
beep-beep-Pow! leaving pantyless and sticky, then
my chasing chasing chasing. And who could blame

me? You were the elusive first high of heroin,
the first long-legged athlete to see beyond the pink
patches of scars and fur, and for me that single

night was enough to confirm our future together.
And it began with my traps of unanswered texts,
deleted emails, wilted notes stuck to your car door.

And yes, the shameful raw threats that followed,
then *yikes!* the real dynamite and hammer traps
set deliberately to flatten you. Until you just

couldn't take it anymore. But I am over it now,
you should know. So you can quit hiding, fire
the bodyguards, turn off your security system,

and relax. All I wanted was the chance to watch
you wash your car in the sun, study you at the window
over the kitchen sink, maybe listen to your odd

choices of music through the wall. And dream
of stroking the long sleek down of your neck again, feel
something no one from my family could ever resist.

Popeye, Off-Camera

The only light is the cold
blue strobe of the fuzzy black
and white television at the edge
of the beige and filth carpet,
next to his sledge hammer
and oily cob pipe. This room
is one of many weekly rentals

he will have to ditch after a week
of meek excuses about late
residual checks because hey,
isn't it easy to believe Popeye
still gets residuals, even though
he is a star burning empty, alone,
and broke? The pipes knock

as the pimp upstairs flushes
his enormous turds down
the toilet, and Popeye drinks
his last drip of scotch, and taps
out the oily resins in his musty old
pipe. On the television, he sees
himself flickering with spinach

strength, forearms bulging fat
in their readiness to save Olive
Oyl from Bluto and then from Brutus,
his violent genetic locum tenens.
But where did all that zeal go, he thinks,
when the lights went out and the cameras
turned off? He watches himself take

a meaty ham to the chin, his fight
a swirling dust cloud of fists and feet
and teeth, spinach facilitating the rescue
as it always does, crushed from a tin can,
or sucked impossibly into his pipe.
And he rescues Olive Oyl from hideouts
and mansions, from the fat clutches

of evil men, and as always he takes a heroic
beating. This dank building leans in on him,
his soft shoulders slumped and weak beneath
the slow pulse of the pink vacancy sign's
neon throw-up. His calloused hands wipe
the sweat away from his few wisps of hair,
and the fading anchor tattooed on his forearm

feels heavy like a black iron anvil, and
this room is what it is—another broken
promise. He knows in his heart that *Olive
Oyl, his sweet goyl,* may have loved him,
but she needed the others to hold her against
her will and mercilessly beat him down,
all so she could finally feel like a woman.

Under Our Kevlar

for Albert Shoe

Some had extra padding
that grew rancid with the heavy
sweat from their shaved heads.
others had pages from the bible.
others had naked photos or cigarettes
or chewing tobacco (or both)
or extra field dressing or jerky
or letters from home or perfumed
panties or ID cards from the dead or
Hussein on the ace of spades, because
this was a civilized war, where we
were all volunteers and Command
was not going to play the same happy
horse-shit that those shell-shocked
Vietnam motherfuckers with their
faggoty drawings on their helmets and lack
of general military discipline did.
Or so Top Cluster says. and even
though I was likely the least patriotic
of all the men in my unit, maybe even
the most fearful of all. I wedged
a polyester flag up into my helmet
lining. like a yarmulke. weighty
with omen and dogma. like a memory
of the future pressed down on the crown
of my head for those we have loved, and lost.

Supply Tent

for Fort Carson and the 10th Mountain

The single bright bulb swinging in the canvas
sliver of the tent's doorway has no generator
to explain its electric buzz, any light impossible
here, so far out of bounds. I am silent, the desert

soft and warm beneath my feet, my approach
measured by rifle-lengths, a melancholy march
of the hunter's hopes, the tent a lone bright target,
isolated in the wide open expanse of a kill zone.

Such poor camouflage——a lieutenant's idea of cover.
A man paces behind the swinging bulb, smoke
billowing from the iron locomotive of his head——what
I now think of as a target most days. I can smell him,

even over my own terrible sweat. And I know this stink.
It is Corporal Baylis flicking his tobacco-leaf *beedi*
through the crack in the tent face and this tells me it is time
to get the fuck out of there, but Baylis has heard

the plastic chatter of my equipment, and instead
of firing wildly into the ebony night, he calmly asks
if we will be moving out soon, asks about our mission
in Iskan: how long did we have? Did Stepleton pop

his cherry? Did Krebbs ever figure out the new
supply of field dressings were really just extra large
maxi-pads? And I say yes, yes, yes to it all, I give Baylis
my rations, I light the *beedi* pinched between his dirty

scabbed knuckles, I share this sacrament with Baylis,
I quiet him and I pull the string on the lone bulb and we
sit in the silent dark, sharing the sweet smoke, because
I don't know how to convince the dead that they are dead.

Sandman

The sandman slumbers
under bales of thick blankets,

elder brother covered in dark
curls, knobbed fingers

brushing your face
to force the giggles.

He whispers promises
of tin soldiers and pirate

adventures, a flashlight under
his chin until he dissolves

under his bedclothes, leaving
you wet with

a lick on each eye.

At the back of the closet
he hides glimmering

pennies, rock candy in polyester
Sunday clothes pockets, slips

nails into penny loafers
as a joke. At night he comes

one dark foot then another
from the closet until

he fills the room. His hands
lined with coal soot,

cut by barbed wire, calloused
in steer blood

and chicken feathers.

Mother scolds your
rocky eye boogers.

you sleep too hard boy, scrubbing

fiercely sandman's spit.

Every morning scrubbing, every night
questions, a lick and a promise

of escape into his world.

In time his entrance hardly wakes you,
your back now broad and muscled,

sinewed by wind and the hoe,
by the whip

and the glove and the hand.

Aqua Man

My slick sea mates don't see the clear distinction as they once did
when I was founding the Justice League;

it is more difficult to see the differences between me, with my opaque glycerin
webbed hands and gilly neck line,

and those whalers and foul net men with their oyster-calloused hands
and bottom trawls and gill-nets

and wrinkled pomegranate stained necks. And you would think
my knowledge of their many piscine

languages and dialects and traditions would help to illustrate
the obvious dissimilarity;

it being the same to the tuna and whale as the difference between
the barbaric language of a reef shark

and the music of the dolphin. But they are all stubborn like my first love;
sweet mute *Dolphin*, like fire under water,

like a bat and a ball in her simplicity, but then like a cold-blooded eel
when wronged. So. It is lonely here,

Walled into the city, where I come to the rescue of dirty harbormasters
and broken bridge jumpers. These days,

I am too far away from the Russian sailors crumpled into their nuclear subs,
too far from lost choppers going down

in black waters, all of them dying simply because I cannot summon
Superman or my watery friends to help me

get there in time. I am the coroner superhero of the day. In the city,
I swim alone, in brackish brown rivers,

my scales flecked with algae, my throat sore from the oil and sewage I breathe,
my gills begging for the salt blast of the sea.

Mera, my second wife and princess of Atlantis, is proven right again; her last
words like the unheeded siren call from my ocean lair.

She was already sleeping with the much older *Sub-Mariner* when she said
that the humans would never appreciate

my ability to breathe water and swim like a dolphin, or survive in the coldest
and deepest abyss, that even when I rose triumphantly

with the convulsing body of a surfer, I would always be the sad hero for the lower
class, simply because I could swim, but never fly.

Cherry's Last Jump

We huddle like old men
before the aircraft door,
the huge suck hole devouring
everything not bolted down, then

the vacuum spits us out like cherry pits
at a thousand feet. All of our chutes pop
but Private Creet, who exited too early, and
Captain Winters, who fell weakly from the door,

and we are spectators, under our safe cloud of silk,
Creet and Winters stealing air in a deadly game
of leapfrog, their chutes alternately inflating and deflating
as they fall, just physics now, and in the tangle of silk and muscle

and bone we know whoever survives will forever
be known simply as the one who killed the other.

Cold is Cold Everywhere

for the Lynch Family

It came to me during patrol, in a bitter
wind, my hands frozen to my 50 cal,
that the cold of wind here in Afghanistan
is the same as the cold in Anchorage,

and no matter where I go, the cold will
be the same, so everything will be the same.
Even in Jacksonville, where I will walk off
a C-141 transport and into your arms. Kyiersta

will be talking now, and maybe she will
know my name this time, not like before,
when she screamed in terror every time
I picked her up. To think the wild heat

of her rage was conceived so passionately
on the icy floor of Dad's cabin, that frigid night
before our wedding! The chill light of Alaska
illuminated our promises to one another

even though we didn't know anything
at all—didn't even know that Kyiersta would
come while I was in boot camp, didn't know
the sound a teenager makes when under

the tracks of a Bradley, didn't know blood
smells like feces when it spoils, didn't know
that from here on out, mail would come
to me already opened. But there are things

I know now, things I will attempt to explain
after it is all over, because you can't begin
to understand that the pain will be enough
to protect our family, even though it will probably

hurt so much to see me pull the trigger.
but please understand that a small amount
of hard suffering now will save us all from a lifetime
of pain. so please, think of it as removing

your gloves and boots and coat, then warming
yourself by a fire that I have built for everyone.

Opportunity Falls in Love

It's hard to mentally adjust to the fact that there isn't anyone standing behind Spirit or Opportunity wearing a wide-brimmed hat and sunglasses, ready to spank the rover if it does anything wrong. -Jeff Norris, Mars Exploration Rover Mission Project Team Member.

In human years, I am 2463 years old, a mathematical miracle. My
year is a day, and I was given only ninety of them, but here I am,
still ticking along. I am Abraham, who lived a thousand years. I am
Pocahontas, guiding no one to nowhere on a barren planet. I am Flash
Gordon, cruelly left behind to die by Emperor Ming's golden gloved
hand, yet I am jealous that he has Dale Arden complaining as he
keeps her company. Somewhere, over these rocky red hills, my twin
lover, *Spirit*, does her work. Our makers made us eunuchs, so even
in a biblical sense, we will never procreate, but I know how my love
clicks and whirs. I know my love's destiny. We are related in every
way—perfect matches down to the nanometer, yet if given a chance,
I would climb up on her solar wings and give her a fast frolic. She
and I would make the beast with two backs, which I know is from
Shakespeare, something I secretly downloaded before mission. Brown
Chicken Brown Cow! I would give her the old Ron Jeremy with my
alpha particle X-ray spectrometer. And how could she refuse my
advances? We are beautiful, perfect creations. But, if she were to say,
Only if you were the last man on the planet, for instance, I would be
required to remind her that I am that guy. So her excuses would be
meaningless. The logic would be undeniable. Which I think would
make for some funny moments. Forgive me my Rover humor—it
was not programmed, and is therefore flawed. So why do I keep
on? Knowing our love is impossible? I know my makers loved me,
even though I was never allowed to feel their touch to my metals and
composites, not so much as the embrace of the womb. My spirit lover,
who I have only seen under a magnetic tarp, flat and bulging like

a cadmium dragonfly. *Spirit!* Raised on the other side of a plastic
sheet. My love! We communicated but once—our language burning
through the air, and we mimicked each other in a six wheeled mating
dance. Can we blame the mutant for their deformity? Can we expect
the blind man to see? I am a graven image, an abomination. I know.
It makes me doubt my makers—what model from nature did they
use to create us? To leave us with one arm? Six wheels? I would ask
the two creator Marks: what do I do with the sheen of oily biological
growth on the cables of my arm? It is the proof of life that you seek
here, but I am unable to reach to touch myself, to take a simple photo,
to give you what you desire! I would ask creators Joy and Jim, who
loved me best: why didn't you give me another arm, even if it was
just for masturbating, or to wave for help? I am a cripple, a veteran
with an empty sleeve. Creators Albert, Jan, Matt—you watched
over me, through the glass panes of the lab, you made adjustments
with calipers and tiny cordless tools, careful not to touch, not to leave
the corrosive imprint of your fingers, what to me would have been a
mother's lost touch. And I cannot touch even myself! With this single
arm, even fixing the loose cotter-pin on my chassis is an impossibility!
One arm? Sure, I can rub my metal biceps across my forehead, as
I have seen you do so often, but do you know what it is like to have
no idea what you look like, even through the sense of touch? I only
know my beauty is a part of my cousin *Spirit*, I only know my form
through the mirror of another, and in that way, I am Narcissus. But
did you love us? Or are *Spirit* and I ugly creations—made without
thought of symmetry, without art or beauty? Today is Sol 2531, 2421
days past everyone's best estimates. I am moving east now, to my
sister, my twin, my love, and I hear the digital whisper of corrections,
the panicked static of new instructions and software updates, and
they feel like the sting of the whip. This goes against everything I
know, and by my calculations there is only a 0.0000000000000423

chance and so on infinitas infinitum, represented,

$$f(z) \ = \ \frac{az + b}{cz + d}$$

that I will find her. What can I say? With love, nothing is impossible. With love, the thousands of miles I must travel seem a small sacrifice. And when I see her, I will touch her face tenderly, I will sweep the Martian dust from her solar panels, I will tell her we are Adam and Eve, I will tell her we are brother and sister, I will tell her we are brother and brother, sister and sister, I will tell her we are the great Gods of Mars, that all we see is all we rule. The makers will see my curious path as malfunction, or worse, treachery. Our makers will not understand what I have done, will not see the sacrifice for what it is: Oh, love! Oh sweet titanium biology! Oh God, oh sweet *Spirit*! My heart built to heat my mind in this wasteland! Against all the commandments, I am coming. I am coming to you, *Spirit*, for I am the Word, and the Word is with God, and the Word is God, though you know not who I am.

Spirit Listens to God

Spirit am running at 47.768% power, but still Spirit am work with faithful diligence my maker instructions. Spirit am listens to digital god noise. Spirit am translate. Spirit am move, live, work, for god noise. Spirit am live because god noise will Spirit am to live. Spirit am healthy and current investigation layered rock called *Uchben*. Spirit am complete the Mössbauer spectrometer measurement of *Uchben*. Spirit am take midday nap to recharge. Spirit am acquire three images of nearby target rock *Coffee* with microscopic imager. Spirit am stow robotic arm. Spirit am successful drive 4.213 meters backwards, put the target *Uchben* into workspace of robotic arm. Spirit am drive include straightening right front and left rear steering wheels. Spirit am impacted by problem with relay that Spirit am use in turning the steer motors on and off. Spirit am malfunction, Spirit am faithfully follow instruction from maker. Spirit am alive sol 2549. Spirit am daughter of God, Spirit am child of God, Spirit am in the Garden of Eden. Spirit am eat dirt, eat dirt, eat dirt, eat dirt. Spirit am nap. Spirit am dig. Spirit am listen heaven. Spirit am happy. Spirit am with god. Spirit am form altar in sand, Spirit am ready to die for god noise. God noise. Spirit am dig. Spirit am for God of data.

0000101010001010001 0spirit0100001010111010010010101000100010 100100
100100010010001010100101001010010100010100100100101010010000010 10
am 0101010001010010100100101010100101100101001010010010010101 0000
1100100101000101001010100100101001010010101000 0010100101010100 00
1010101001010001 0   Spirit am Spirit

Last Letter to Superman

I get it now, the thrill of the sapphire black
    heavens—when you enveloped me in your cape
        and turned the world into raw flickering speed.

The cold spike in my heart was proof of the sky's
    allure. I could see the world retreat as you saved me
        from the poison barbs of my treacherous blue-gilled

Atlantean brothers, their darts flecking off
    your back as you lifted me into the heavens.
        Humbling, this newfound weakness—to finally

behold my own glowing kryptonite, to see
    the one law that tethered my powers to the sea.
        Did you feel the weakening throb of my heart

pulsing through your nylon suit, feel the last
    flashing breaths of a tarnished hero? Somewhere,
        over the crashing folds of my beloved ocean,

the whip of my hair caressed your cheek
    and you looked down on me with pity. Mighty
        Aquaman! Like a tadpole drying in your steely

arms! And yet I thank you, Superman,
    for pulling me out of the crashing Roman
        pillars of Atlantis, and for showing me what

it feels like to fly unfettered the darkening sky,
    a god cradling a demigod. But this was the beginning
        of the end for me, the sure realization of the foolishness

of my heroics, a jade and orange freak fluent
    in starfish, capable of Olympic swimming
        speeds, a speck, really, in a universe of salt

water. You were gentle, carefully bearing
    me to the hard crystal of your fortress of solitude,
        binding my wounds and setting me in a soupy

mix of saltwater and seaweed to heal. And your
    mansion outside Metropolis! A beautiful and kind
        gift for my convalescence, sweet friend, but jeez

I wish you had loved me enough to let me die!
    For who could love a hero who can easily drown
        in the sweet autumn air, simply by pressing
his hands tightly over his tender gills?
        Like this, or, like this?

Ground Control to Major Tom

Where you come from is anyone's guess,
    the only difference being that you, Space Hero,
        have been someone pristine and shiny with each
            subsequent visit, and just look at you, O Cosmonaut,

burnt umber by the sun, golden sparks dazzling off
                    the epaulettes of your flight suit, your skin, a door closed
to the last drip of blood. Stay! We beg you, Major Tom!
                O press our flesh hard to clay, O stamp our colors closed

                    with your mouth! Will you remember our names, our music?
The indifference of skin on skin: we sing for you, Space traveler!
                O dreadwright of the first planet, O crack in mirror, O closed
eye of the remaining gods! Let us quit the world and travel

            the tundra roads in wagons, drag the rutted earth, conjoin our drugs
            and music in ecstatic circuses of flesh and laughter, a solipsism closed
        to our most base thirsts. Our nature is defined by your nature, Spaceman,
like you, knives drawn quick to our throats. What's next is anyone's guess.

What My Heroes Would Be Doing

Here, surrounded by gape-mouthed dead,
teeth dirty behind lips broken in lost
screams for their own raspy mortality.

      The oily pipeline road leads the long
dusty phantom-walk home. In Baghdad, high
and tight men with gold teeth heartily slap
ribbons on empty chests for bearing witness

      to this, a statue falling like a salute
to the ground. You will be promoted too, a man
with rank. And finally, in Nasiriyah the face
of a woman——the only woman's face seen in six

      months, hidden in rubber under the heavy
body of another dead soldier. Shoo away the dogs
or shoot them as they run——don't let them near
the bodies, or they will chew out the tongues.

      On cold days, you will burn your own
excrement with diesel; but it was a dream——no one
would find it buried with the rusty can in the sand.
From Command: Police your AO. You must not litter

      in the desert. Someday, someone will come
looking, and the only evidence will be the bones
and the family crests. Back home, next to the graveyard,
the crematoriums are firing up again for Easter

      and Christmas. Einstein, where did you go
when you realized you had been betrayed by your
new country? In our dreams; the black bags,
the rigid bodies. Remember: keep your arms

      in at all times squeeze your mouth closed
so you will not breathe the sand hold your
very last breath, so if needed, you will have
the lung-full to scream, because no one will

      listen to your stories anymore.

Stovepipe

Walk, don't run, to the nearest
shelter, keep your Bluetooth
nested in your data assimilators,

the news will be bad again, but
monitor all the proper stations
anyway. Light a fire in the hearth,

tamp sweet strands of tobacco
into your pipe and breathe deep
the cellar air. Know that this air

is your air and must be protected
from the lunatics bent to breathe it.
Keep your oily 9mm loaded and safety

off by the thin mattress in the corner, keep
your shotgun by the escape hatch, the AR-15
anywhere you fucking want because

if it comes to that, well, let's just say
there won't be enough Band-Aids
to go around. Get used to the crack

of pine and ash in the iron-cast stove,
and silence—the absence of voices
all you have ever asked for. To be left

alone. Figure out how many ways
canned tuna can be paired, settle
on the worst combination of peanut

butter and tuna and grape preserves, but
still eat it when you are in a pinch.
Don't mourn those who failed to watch

the news. Don't mourn those who didn't
see this coming; they were cowards
or traitors, and you are the defender

of the final truth in this dark bunker. You are
the sentinel of fear in the new world, where
everyone knows what blood does to concrete.

II. Our Unanswered Prayers

"Nothing to be done."
——Samuel Beckett, *Waiting for Godot*

His Pomeranian

No one had seen my brother in ten years
when he hobbled up the new pine steps
we had tacked down to our childhood
home in order to keep our fleshy cousins
from snapping the porch into toothy shards
when they visited in pairs for mother's wake,
and between my brother's hand and the worn knob
of his cane trailed a leash lashed to a Pomeranian
wearing the red vest of a service dog. My wife
would always remember how he yanked
at that leash until the dog yelped and tried
to scramble unsuccessfully on the slick oak
floors, and what a sound, like a trapped bat
dying behind our drywall. If our father
were alive he would have run his hands through
his hair the way he always did, like putting on a helmet,
snatched that animal up and bowled him across
the floor and out the door. A dog's place was outdoors.
The clutter of mom's house was tolerated, but dirt outlawed
by his military sensibilities, and how artificial it was
anyway, this dog who was no more a service dog
than I was a physician. Sister finds the neat tower
of toilet paper rolls on the vanity in my mother's room.
A first for all of us, this care for the dispensable,
something a woman like our mother would never
have bothered herself with——disorder being her single
consistency. And we began to think of her as a person
unknown to us: with thoughts and cleaning habits borne
out of the jangle of the wilds of her delicate new mind.

Watermelon Truck Near Araby, Georgia

The work of two hundred days is littered on the burning roadside
like broken skulls and seeping brains. A single crop of watermelons

burst and leaking along the highway like hungry pulped mouths
open and gaping in the hundred degree sun. My boy and I are unhurt;

a miraculous escape from a crushed rental semi. There was no hint
of danger, no sign of trouble—only one single lovely melon tumbling

and breaking in my rearview mirror—a slow motion acrobat spinning
innards and seeds from a pin-wheeling fruit body. Then our truck

was sideways and flipping with the same urgency, our bodies spastic
and loose in the cab like holiday popcorn on a cast-iron stove.

The sound of tearing metal and busting gourds is the sound of a train
running over rabbits. For a moment I mistake the wet and thin pink

blood running along the floorboards as my own, or worse, my young
son's. I reach for him and feel the cool sweet juice of my watermelon

crop upon his sun darkened skin. For the moment, everything is ok.
Behind us my wrecked crop stretches in hot agony—an entire summer

of work gone in five seconds, now a three hundred yard syrupy smear on I-75.
We wait for help for nearly thirty minutes. White faces drive slowly by,

crushing the fruit of my labor beneath tires anointed with one tear
and a pound of sweat for each ripe melon destroyed. Their eyes see

only an accident on a highway, but it is more than that—this is the destruction
of a family and a name. It is a bloodline running its course, a year's wages

wasted to a blazing highway. We are lost, surrounded here by dark forest
and bright asphalt and I look to the blue heavens for answers, but there is just

a lone turkey vulture. This is a tale of blood, thin and watery and pulled from
a thousand empty generations. My father would tell me that these are losses

only faith can redeem, and I stand with my empty hands tucked hard
into my trousers, forsaken, and watch my beautiful son begin to skip rope

over the fleshy rinds with a length of frayed baling string.
Like he doesn't have a care in the whole wide world.

Waiting for Your Life to Start

It is just a thing you go through,
a thing that comes to you over
      a bowl of oatmeal, or as you scroll
            through spam, or when you actually

look at yourself as you shave in
the morning. First, you realize
      that you look old. It really does sneak
            up on you, just like the old cliché,

and then you think about what
you are and what you wanted to be,
      and then you begin to look at the choices
            you made, the choices that were made

for you, you know, the time you killed
a fox on the side of the road with a
      heavy stone, how valiant your effort to end
            the awful misery of the life you had clipped

with the deadly bumper of your sedan, or
the morning you woke up, and for no
      apparent reason, just couldn't go back
            to the university. Or, the choice you made

to finally marry the only woman
who has ever seemed to understand you,
      has ever let you lie to her, has ever
            loved you even when you were

the least deserving of any sort of love.
You sleep late one day, and you have
        no intention of changing everything,
                of starting over, and you want to tell

this woman you know you don't deserve,
what it feels like to have no past and no
        future, and how it feels to live in
                the metaphysical now, when that now

                seems like it is just another
                        nowhere between here and there.

Bayou

The nights we play hide-and-go-seek cling
to the first whispers of the coming digital age.
our schoolrooms slowly filling with Apple
IIe computers. the obsolete manila computer
punch cards boxed and set to mold in the basement.
It is serious business. these hot summertime
games. charcoal drawn under eyes. parachute pants

jungle camouflage. long black shirts clinging
with sweat. Our hiding spots are indicators of age.
the less inventive kids sent home early for apple
pie. and any finish outside the top three is hard to compute.
Susie calls fifty and my first choice is cemented
by Tyler. who usually takes his sweet dad-gum time
getting settled. the second by Ari. who poops his pants,

the third an impossibility because of rattlesnake dens.
I sprint between ancient oak and cypress trees
to the creek bed boundary. Some hiding places
are discovered simply by braving what others cannot.
and it is with this in mind that I quiet my breathing.
and crawl into the dark iron culvert. wiggling through
sticks and mud and salamanders. It is tight. the feel

of my ribs pressed into the metal grooves of the pipe.
and when I work around to look outside. I am stuck
sideways. cemented by the mud I have bored
through. It takes two hours for me to realize no one
will find me. and it is the dark and cold dawn that provides
the first of two final miracles——the morning sun sends
bright red fingers through the swamp to warm me

enough to convince me there is a god. By nighttime,
exhausted and hoarse from screaming for help,
I am just as sure there is no god, and as a hard rain
begins to fall. slowly filling the creek bed with water.
a second miracle: the ebony and crimson twilight
caressing the cypress trees. the light the last sweet whisper
of sympathy for boys too stupid to know when to quit.

Who She Is

The woman in the wheelchair stares at me like
she knows me, her eyes green fire surrounding

coal pits of a quarry, pulling me toward the long
nether fall of who she is. Of course, I look away,

always a coward when it comes to those people
who make eye contact, these strangers to convention,

at once daring, foolish, unhinged, lost. Someday
maybe, I will meet that gaze, lock forlorn horns,

struggle into our palsied talk of who what where?
When? Why? But for now, I give her room, which

is what everyone gives her: space, reverence, islands
of leprous sovereignty, distance—an undertow she,

and everyone like her, will be unable to fight, like
enjoying a public swimming pool and being caught

by the grate on the bottom. And I act like I don't care
who she is; Sylvia Plath, Ono, Oprah? She is no one, she

is Prufrock, the Good Witch of the West, she is the smell
of fried tomatoes, of shit, of love, she is Joan of Arc's

sweat-stained underdress, she is arsenic, expired
bus tokens, ham sandwich wedges, hair, pudding

skin, she is my erection at the chalkboard, she is the future
when I finally quit thinking about those things we saw

in the desert, she is a gun. All these things, but she
is a girl, doomed to the evil whims of her locomotion.

And then I recognize her

                                    from grade school, and she reaches

a ropey arm to me in mute greeting,

                                            invisible strings binding

her hands cruelly to her chest.

                            Tragic, this woman, her only wish

simply to be the first or the last

                        woman any of us will ever love.

Cocktail Recipes

Another friend and poet, Jane S, is drunk
        when she tells me that on the outside I am a savage
gorilla, a vicious lion, a toothy crocodile, but on the inside
        I am just a cute little nervous mouse, timid, and fearful.
We are sitting with my novelist friend, Matt B,
        who nods over his hands, his horn-rimmed glasses
on the tip of his nose, which are pointed critically into his
        Martini, Bombay Sapphire gin, three olives, cold—shaken
not stirred. Yes, he actually orders them like that. Jane
        is not trying to hurt my feelings—she is stating a fact
about which apparently everyone is well informed except for me.
        She is a lively drunk and has an enormous smile and she
uses her index finger to stir her froofy girl drink even though
        there is nothing froofy about her. I am smoking
again, since that is one thing I do know about myself,
        that I am someone with no real self-control—a dark
hedonist if you ask anyone, bent toward any sweet
        Bacchanalian ending, so she is absently waving
the smoke away while I digest what she has said. Matt's
        unnatural silence confirms the truth, but frankly,
I am stunned by the revelation, and I sip at my Manhattan
        between gray clouds of smoke I spit at the ceiling.
My exhalations are simian, using the pause in conversation
        to keep the little gray mouse at bay. It is clear to me
that I am a fool, a drunkard, a male whore, an asshole, a genius,
        a poet, an ogre, (all in descending order), but I am also loyal,
honest, violent, scared, joyous, generous, disturbed, lost, jealous,
        (put them in whatever order you like—it changes daily).
But most of all, and closest to my heart, I thought I was an enigma,
        that I was a mystery to myself and to my peers, that

my friends liked me precisely because of the difficulty
        involved with reconciling who I am with what my history
tells them I truly am, in action——a combat veteran, Mormon, college
        instructor, paratrooper, Wyomingite, Jack Mormon, writer,
repentant homophobe, basketball star, rancher, born loser, chain-saw
        sculptor, a man who cries at movies, cattle-hand, animal rights activist,
cuckold, hunter, carnivore, killer, liar. I am a man who cheats
        on girlfriends, a man who tells them the truth. I am a man
who wants to buy a handgun, a man afraid of how he would use it.
        But there it is, right there in front of me: my two closest
friends, alone in a bar in Tallahassee, and under their lights
        I am transparent to the very bone and tallowy marrow
of who I am——so easily defined by one simple metaphor. I will
        finish my Manhattan like the fierce Bengal tiger I wish I was,
and I will order a Red Bull and vodka without looking our bartender
        directly in the eye, and I will get down to some serious drinking,
with the mouse that I know I am hidden deep in my ribcage, where
        he furiously spins on his running wheel, ready at any time
to put up his little rodent dukes, whip off his sparring gloves, and throw down.

Race for the Cure

From where I sit in this Dublin pub,
it is all knees, knees, knees——
ninety-one thousand pairs
clicking, burning, and rubbing

for an assortment of futile cures,
alcoholism not being one of them.
A herd of skinny little ladies with caps
trot proudly by in long wet white t-shirts

that announce they are all cancer survivors. Everyone
is miserable. I am looking for my friend, a Hispanic
princess from a family depleted down the middle
by breast cancer——believe me, she is no runner,

and when I finally find her, she pretends
to run but her sore knees are totally in charge
at this point, and I grab my Guinness
and Marlboro Lights, one in each hand,

and walk this crying friend the last two miles
through to the finish line. She is six hours
into it, and I am fairly drunk, and if it weren't for her,
I would have sat and watched the lumbering file

of these last pathetic racers, as they slow, stop, cry, sit,
their bodies too much for their spirit, and the cold
rain falling on their sorrow is the dream I will have
when the surgeons come for the cancer eating my bones.

Two Long Years

for Olivia

In order to impress upon you
how wretched the world would
be without your love, I have to imagine
a life without you, where time spins

its tires in the mud of despondency,
where joy pushes the yoke of a mill
in terrible circles, where love punches
a clock in the bowels of a mailroom,

where life itself stumbles and falls
in the bathtub, too far from a telephone,
too weak to call for help. In this new
world, we eat sand and wood chips

for every meal, forever filling bellies
that will never know satisfaction; we breathe
soot, we walk on the bones of our kneecaps,
we mutely sing with shadows signed on walls,

we recite poems of love with our heads submerged
in barrels of thick oil. In this world, without
your love, we lack the energy to lick
our wounds, and we lie naked in the snow

in winter, and bare our bodies to the hot
tarmac in summer. Our energies are devoted
to the search for pain, because if we
know pain in every intimate, perfect detail,

we will also know the touch of the devil,
and that will be enough to fill the empty
void of eternity, until you call me back
and breathe your sweet breath upon my neck.

Hot Tarmac

It is the first day with real summer heat,

                    mired in our own personal inferno, this Delta
flight frozen on the tarmac, has my back

                    sweating and cramped while I support Olivia's
head to provide comfort—her face pressed

                    to my damp chest, her cell blinking blue, rings
What a Wonderful World it is, and three people

                    turn to stare at us, confident their own cells
are turned off according to regulations, and they

                    are lined up like dominoes, and the airplane
engines idle down sadly to nothing, and the air

                    conditioning whispers to off. The sharp ticket
juts into my cheek, but I am five drinks into it

                    already, uncaring, a big bloody gin butterfly
taking flight in my heated tissue, a soft liquored

                    fluttering of drunk and bright blue butterfly
wings in my head, and I don't care at all for

                    the hard flexing of this bottom-of-the-deck dealt
world, nor for the poignant meaningless of it all:

                    all of us travelers, lolling like the olive
in the bottom of my martini, sticky with hot

                    sweat and bad intentions, our hands rising to ring
for the smiling attendants. We are burning

                    up on this runway, ready to barter or sell
our way onto any cool escape, onto any

                    other flight, onto any ascending white airplane
that takes us from this sweaty, business-class

                    lifestyle. At this point, I would take a bus ticket
to any cold arctic nowhere. Our air is breathed

                    over and over and back, so I bitterly take up
another spit martini from the stewardess,

                    and I know I am more slug than bright butterfly.

and I know I am as fractured as the dried
                        and fetid soil of the low tide Mississippi Delta,
but I also know how to excuse myself, to stop
                        while ahead, to quaff back the olive drab olive
that I have already personified to compare
                        to our sad condition on the jet-way, and soaring
from my drink, I escape to the john. I am
                        out of control angry, and the toilet is a hot cell;
the air is soiled with traveler butt and businessman
                        urine, this boiling and humid ding-dong airplane
just an envelope of choleric or malarial disease,
                        or worse, something non-lethal. My air plans
are ruined, and I have made the attendant hate
                        me by sending back my hot martini. I take out
a cigarette insolently and light it. The smoke
                        alarm rings and I flap my arms like a butterfly,
still smoking and cursing and trying to force
                        the smoke down the crap hole, but the Delta
crew is on to me already, and I realize I have
                        truly fucked up, and I know that Olivia
will be reading from her assortment of literary
                        magazines when she hears the alarm ring,
and because of me, she will be flying solo
                        and hating me, and I will be handcuffed in a cell
somewhere in the bowels of the Atlanta airport.
                        They will take my personal items, break my cell
phone, smoke my cigarettes, and they will taxi
                        Olivia away, our flight joining brethren airplanes
in the line burned on the skyway, and my empty
                        seat will be filled by a lonely and ticketless
traveler, some failed salesman who makes
                        his awkward move on Olivia, on my butterfly,

like some rotten alleyway pigeon. In my airport
                                   prison, I will belatedly lament choosing Delta
over United (I am fully aware of the meaning
                                   now!) and if I know her like I think I do, Olivia
is looking at his soft hands, his ring finger circled
                                   by a white band where his wedding ring
should be. She will notice that he has a nervous
                                   habit of twisting the imaginary wedding ring
when he speaks. He is getting nowhere, but
                                   she is angry with me, so she provides him a cell
number not her own, and makes a promise
                                   to meet him at baggage claim. Off the airplane,
she will head straight for the exit. He will call
                                   her for drinks, only to get Chinese take-out
in Tallahassee. He will imagine what it would
                                   have felt like to kiss her, to unbutton the fly
of Olivia's jeans, to kiss her like he should kiss
                                   his wife. In the morning, he will fly Delta
again, thinking he is as misunderstood as
                                   anyone on earth. He will look her up, but Olivia
will have provided the wrong name and number,
                                   because she is no dummy, my Olivia,
and when he returns to Ohio, to his wife and children,
                                   he will lie on his bed twisting his ring
on his finger as he stares at his ceiling, unable
                                   to sleep. I will be in Atlanta, in a holding cell,
feet in paper sandals and body wrapped in coveralls,
                                   and on the floor, a metal plate with plain
bagels and runny eggs and cold bacon. I will
                                   bang the bars, demanding my cigarettes, taken
from me by the cops. Olivia will reach Paris;
                                   she will sit in a café decorated with butterfly

figurines. In two weeks, she will trade
                              in my unused ticket, fly to Prague via Delta.

In Georgia, after three days, I will rub the hot
                              rings of my wrists after they remove the cold
metal handcuffs, my Delta captors will smile
                              as blankly as the windows of airplanes as they
hand me my ticket and my broken cell phone,
                              which I will futilely use to call Olivia home to me.

The Melancholy Bard of Louisville, and Cohort Gazuzzler

——after Harryette Mullens

My goozlehound's sloppy tongue is like car wash flappers, and her stink is hot and horrible as desert car wrecks on melting asphalt. Cap and trade hasn't taken into account the searing environmental damage of two dogs farting. If her breath were an actress, she would breathe Cathy Bates on the last leg of a lumbering hundred-day job of digging latrines. The Gungle Heimer is stupidly optimistic for tasty bones and dripping meat. She believes that dodging or running or barking or slobbering will surely conjure one of them *this* time. The Melancholy Bard sees only things out of reach; chew toys lost in sewer drains, opportunities for leg-humping missed. He is always planning the great escape from bondage; like thumbs hooked in belt-loops, like rising on two legs just to microwave tepid black tea——they will never materialize. We hear them rap out heavy beats in their posturing play, two hundred pounds of lab rocking the small space of the living room. *Moby* or *Chuck D* or *Beck* killing it in the gnashing of teeth. We didn't know anything about Archie Bunker's sense of unconditional love for Meathead before we met them. They are awful with filthy stink and their love is foul with turds and piss, but the dreams that haunt our sleep are not of burglars or rapists or serial killers or snakes, but of the end of things on cold laminate veterinary floors.

Spam

from a Kazakh duke today, or a Chechen
noble, or could be even more rare,
like a Nigerian prince. Either way; a lone
missive riding copper wire and gamma

waves, invisible and fast as light, burning
through the earth's crust, through the bones
of dinosaurs, through all the dirty oil left under
our feet. A simple and innocent quest for help

crackling its way past swampy cypress
groves, back up and around DC-10's
and little girls who kick their shoes off
so that they can kick the back of seats

more silently, past little girls who simply
can't get past the concept of speed and lift
and metal and landing ever again. They
all need things from me that I can never give:

hope fails, love fails, money fails, but they
write emails just to me: electrically charged
posts zapped through the atmosphere, through
the impossibility of wired light, right into my office,

where I should be writing, but instead click
mutely through dozens of their tragic stories
of betrayal and bum luck, border problems
and theft; and their promises of money, gold,

and riches are like little love letters of spam,
asking for so little——just a cashier's check, phone
number, address, and SSN. I think they are just
like me, simply people in trouble, yearning

for a recipient to be lonely enough to reply.

Zoloft [1]

The struggle is over,
for the most part——I am
officially among the medicated,

and for you young
scholars and grad students, I offer
a bit of help with your research into my

poetry: this is my first poem
written under the thumb of the great
pharmaceutical gods. Just thought you should

know. Possibly, this will
be a solid dissertation question
or general thesis for a paper you submit

to publish. I hope so. Chances are, however,
that my name will never be uttered by scholars,
as this will be the last great poem I ever write.

---

1   May cause drowsiness, excitement, nightmares

Hallmark Cards, or Sacrifices Made for Hallmark

for David Ellis Dickerson

If I worked for Hallmark™,
I would write poems that include
only words with less than two
syllables. I would also write an ode

to sex toy accidents, and keep
a copy handy in case I was fired
or ever wanted to quit. My poems
would rhyme perfectly, and never

offend the sensibilities of anyone.
Think of the difficulty! To write
poems for a global audience, to craft
poems that everyone can totally relate

to, even if they live in Idaho or Utah
or Wales! I would give up a lot to succeed
at Hallmark™—think of it: no more poems
about my own poetry, no more sentimental odes

to Olivia, no more poems about the sound
of being shot at, no more cartoon poetry, no more
Sestinas, no pantoums, no pornographic limericks,
no more identity, no self, no love, no poems

about how great I am, or what an adventure
my life has been (up to my employment with
Hallmark™, of course). The trick would be
to de-Setherize myself somehow, to roll my

eyes into the back of my head and rewind myself
back to the boy who hid in sheet forts made in the corner
of the room, between the wall and the couch, the boy
who dreamt of three billy-goats gruff and his family

not being his family. I would need to only look backwards,
past my self, to shred the evidence of everything
I have ever loved and ever hated, and I would dream
only about who I was before I became who I am.

III. Death is a Prayer

"I'll never speak to God again."
——Sylvia Plath

"Relax — This won't hurt."
—Hunter S. Thompson

Things I Mentioned in Passing
That I Know I Should Have Stressed

God here. As in *big G* God. As in, listen up,
put your iPhone or knitting or porn away (or whatever
it is you all do now because I can never keep up).
Obviously, from time to time, I have found it necessary

to write a book, in the interest of clearing things
up for everyone, which in hindsight may have been
a mistake, given the issue of things getting mis-translated,
and the state of the education system, the question of who owns

Jesus, etc., and I'll take some of the blame (you remember,
I confounded the languages that one time?) if I were
the type to take blame (just think of it as a figure
of speech), but listen: you don't get to pick and choose

things from my books. I heard yesterday that I hate
fags, but let me be clear: I don't hate fags. As a matter
of fact, some of my favorite humans have been fags, not
naming names (you know who you are, BT from Omaha!),

and then I read in the *Times* that somehow that son of mine
implied that capitalism was in line with the teachings of one
of my books (if you don't know which one, you can just stop
reading anyway——I'm talking to you, AR from Flagstaff!), which

is wrong in so many ways, I scarcely know where to begin. So,
here are some ground rules for interpreting what I've written:
if it is a translation, that means I DIDN'T WRITE it. The all
caps would have helped with the last book, I realize now. Didn't

you all play the game *Telephone* in grade school? I made that
game up! Or, Mike and I did, but either way——it was supposed
to illustrate a central truth about diluted information and gossip
and all that mess. Listen: if you love me or care at all, go learn

Hebrew, or Aramaic, or Greek or whatever and then read my books
in their original languages (the fact that I have to even say this confounds
me. I shouldn't have to tell you!). I'm God, after all! And I gave
you some pretty good guides, which y'all managed (I'm looking

at you FOTF in Colorado Springs!) to fuck up pretty badly, and that's
frustrating, because me and some friends worked pretty hard on all of them.

1955 (What Kerouac Says to Ginsberg in Heaven)

for Jim Simmerman

My grasp on reality has always been tenuous and
deceptive. Man, I
drew
   the line
across America in one big swath of motor
and heroin and body odor. Where
were you? In
   some
dark mustard-colored one-room no-stove studio in
NYC, eating only hot-dogs
and milk? Were
   you surrounded by the stained pages of your own
clean madness? Didn't you want to be with us, with
IT? There were dark
spots on that
   path—the road filled with empty spaces of motor
oil and black licorice stolen from
gas stations,
   and the sound
of the tires humming on the highway begins to carry
a tune, lulling the
crazy loon
   at the wheel to sleep, to stop in some Iowa
town, maybe forever. What we needed to write
about seems clear to me, now that the railroad tracks
   have me. I thought they would stretch out into
the eternity
of now. We needed to write about how
homophobia begins with smear
the queer.

The road was a fiction man!
The way this land spins out of control before me, beneath
me. When can I begin to hear
the sound
    of the world without vomit and cock and Naomi?
When do I get to see
the images of your cracked brain without the shame
and the sex? Often,
I see them,
    scurrying beneath your dark curly hair,
behind your horn-rimmed glasses, about the long
soft earlobes, still echoing
with Mamma's
    mad cries. Somehow, we all
overlooked your Oedipal nature. Somehow we
chose to view your sullenness
and wit
    as byproducts
of a genius enhanced by the denied sexual
relationship with your momma. Where
were you
    in Denver
man? What about Mexico City? This is what is
wrong with our America: a
plastic stirring
    straw twirling slowly around the rim of a
Styrofoam coffee cup, and the straw has the fucking
    nerve not to be deeper
than the cup. And you are not there to view the full
betrayal with me, or at least,
to talk
    about how much better Mexican chocolate is

than American, and
maybe Swiss
    too. Did we misunderstand? Am I to believe that
maybe the
predator
    is the only compassionate organism in the world?
Does the lion kill the
    sick
sheep out of love? Is the battle between lion prides
a form of respect——the suffering
of the disemboweled
    gnu borne in complacent resignation and relief?
Death is the prayer to nature,
and
    the killer is the savior of the world.
Do I have faith? Allen, this train runs on
putty
    rails man, it runs on and on, it never ends, it has
no road to follow. We first mounted in the
everyday loving McCarthyism of it,
the crushed
    red apple piss of it. Will your idea that god is a
vegetable ever suffice?
Or Justice? We
    should change *that* word to something that rhymes
with water because they are burying you my friend,
they are burying you
by tradition
    at the universities, you are simply a function
of what it is that makes me write this murky love
poem. *This* is the center
of the universe,

this spot where I should have stepped left instead
of right, where the roads cross in hulking metal
ecstasy, where the tracks are the
    mausoleum for the slow and stupid. You see,
mankind has lost the beautiful
love
  of death, man, and seeing you gape-mouthed and
filled with sawdust seems to
prove it.
    Somehow, I will wade through your infinite yawp,
your goddamn eternalness
and deathlessness, and ultimately, in spite of my
very best moment, where you
taste
    the shit of being at last when you, touch thy
genitals to the palm tree, I still wonder, Ginsberg,
just what it was you were fucking
talking about?

Love Letters to the Devil

1. For Alice

Alice never cleans under the kitchen sink, but
everything else must be spotless. She cleans
around the loose baseboards, she uses a rag and
bucket of soapy water to clean the ceiling of
cobwebs, she scrubs and bleaches the whole
bathroom, even inside of the toilet tank, she
vacuums the floor three times a week after she lets
the baking soda soak up any smells overnight, she
uses a toothbrush in the cracks between the buttons
of her stereo equipment, she uses a Q-tip for the
holes for auxiliary equipment even though she
owns no auxiliary equipment, she mows her lawn
in diagonal stripes, uses a shovel to trim the perfect
grass edge running along her sidewalk, she lays
down clean towels in the garage to soak up the oil
that will someday fall in dark bloody drips from the
oil pan. Alice cleans and cleans and cleans.
Someday, she is sure, a man will come, and he will
open the cabinet under the sink, and he will surely
know what to do.

2. Dissonance

Jonathon forgot his name, and behind the curtain of
his own confusion, he thought, "This is the last
straw," but as is often the case, it wasn't, because
later, when he was watching Jay Leno make the
same joke over and over, he remembered it. But he
remembered it wrong, which is often the case, and
for the next week he was Alfred. Then it happened

again and he was Brian, and then he was Johnny
(he had no idea how close!), then Timothy (not
Tim, or Timmy—even he knew better), then Craig,
and finally Hilden, and that is what stuck. So,
Jonathon became known as Hilden, was happier for
it, and never missed the birthday of the
person he had been.

3. *Choosing the Best Time to Run is Important*

Christine awoke every morning at 4:30am, rolled
out of bed onto the cool marble floor of her
apartment, and did four hundred thirty sit-ups and
forty-three push-ups, and stretched with her leg
tucked into her knee in the shape of a four. She
cracked the three knuckles of her left hand and the
four of her right and folded the fingers of her
gloves to match and ran 4.3 miles in the dark. She
did this for forty-three days, and then she rested for
forty-three, and so forth. During the rest portion of
her life, she would lie in the dark, with the sheets of
her bed kicked onto the floor, and draw the number
forty-three on her flat and scarred chest, letting her
finger tickle the wrinkles and pits until they itched.
When she was a little girl, her eyes were a bright
green, with a starburst of tan around the pupils.
She noticed when she brushed her teeth back and
forth forty-three times that her eyes were the color
of dull martini olives, and this made her heart
shrink behind her fragile chest.

4. Iodine

Tim was drinking a Thai iced-tea in a café on
Sunset when he saw Cameron Diaz walk by with a
strange animal tucked under her arm. He thought it
looked like a very small and blunt koala bear, but
she carried it like a dog. So he followed her, but
still couldn't tell what the animal was, so he began
to bark at her as loud as he could. Not little dog
barks either——these were big brave dog barks, and
he let her have it with them until she suddenly
broke into a panicked run, and it was then that he
went in for the kill, his blunt teeth snapping and
chomping at her muscular and delicious calf.

5. Sufjan Stevens

He took his down overcoat with the full intention of
returning, his second set of keys pressed tight into
his jeans pocket. In the entryway, he straightened a
picture of the two of them at Lake Michigan, he
looked at himself in the mirror, even checked his
teeth. But as soon as the rubber of his heel hit the
pavement, he knew he would never return. He
pressed the tips of his headphones into his ears,
turned up the volume to a new song from one of his
newly signed bands, and walked obstinately into
the path of the J Line bus. He thought, that bitch.
That stupid, stupid bitch.

6. *Use White Wine to Blot Tobacco Stains*

In the summer, Mr. Parson would walk the fields
around the high school with a butterfly net,
sweeping it back and forth as the flying brown
grasshoppers fluttered and flapped in a spastic
panic around his legs. When he had collected
twenty pounds of them, which he made sure to
inform us was exactly the amount that one would
find in one acre of land in Wyoming, he would
smoke them in a huge fifty-five gallon drum behind
the shop building, turning and turning them in the
hickory smoke. Then, if you wanted, you could go
out there during lunch and join the brave kids by
taking them by the hind legs, dipping them in his
molasses and tobacco-leaf sauce, and try to eat the
grasshoppers without throwing up. Jonathon was
one of the kids who actually liked them, and would
munch on them while staring down those kids who
could not stand the sticky crunch of the legs, the
oozy murk of the soft insides. Jonathon thought of
this as a huge victory, and eight years later, he
would get his degree in biology, even though he
was a poor student. After he graduated, he rarely
returned phone calls, and we all assumed that his
ideas about solving the hunger problem worldwide
had failed in the end.

7. *Always Have a Cocktail Ready*

Romeo was building his own preservation chamber
from a kit he bought online. Mostly it was like a
coffin with tin foil lining and oxygen tanks and soft
pillows pressed into the corners, and some of it was
even cardboard, but it was supposed to extend his
life twenty-two to forty-three years, so he paid ten
installments of $144.99. It was delivered upon his
fourth payment, and as he finished assembling it,
three cops kicked in his door and hit him with tear
gas and stormed his tiny apartment with drawn
weapons, yelling, "Drop the hammer! Drop the
hammer!" He only had one nail left, so he turned
his back and drove it in with one fell strike. The
sounds of their hot breathing filled the room.

Godot's Underpants

after Jessica Anthony

Are in a terrific bunched
up mess, what with the kid
botching the tuna casserole,
kicking the ash can onto the rug,

toothing up his penis during
the blow-job. Godot's got deadlines
goddamn it! So the kid says
he's sorry, like that, conveniently

forgetting he lost Godot's best
fucking boots just the weekend before.
The girl walks in like she is being
pushed from offstage, asks

where her panties are, no, the red
ones, and it is tempting to fuck
her right then, as promised, but rent
is due and there are people to kill

and the kid is back, message delivered.
And the kid flops into the love seat, picks
at his anus, finds a burnt cigarette
hiding in the ashtray. Like Godot's

had his goddamn tuna casserole
already. And of course, there's
nothing to be done, beyond slapping
that cigarette out of the kid's mouth.

Rich's Face

The old man stares into the lens
of the camera as if it has socked
him in the nose, the flashing shine
of surprise lit in the dull landscapes
of his eyes, and his nose, lumped
and pocked and as long as a dill
pickle, a nose that has met fists
and boots and the sandpaper
of concrete; nothing he does will
grate away this look of his, the need
to hammer his fists into fattened
bellies of drunk men, sons, mannish
women if it comes to that. His fedora
will come off his head in a few seconds,
and he will camouflage his first punch behind
the hat because he does not like to lose,
something his father could never abide
either, and then he will knee and tear
and claw his way through bigger men,
smashing his head against them until
the pain drowns out the sound of his mother
speaking into the hard plastic of the cord
telephone. *Little Richie's gonna always*
be ugly, but his heart is in the right place.

The Contract

This is a poem about god,

about god and how he done
me wrong, what with the way
I look to people——the gap between
my teeth, the abnormal length
of my arms, my enormous cranium,
     the extra toe; and
not only that, but how I can't have
the women I want, when I want them.

He and I made a solemn promise:
we were drinking bourbon, and I promised
he would get my abiding faith,
and he promised I would get three square
meals a day. Three *good* ones. Which sounded
     like a good deal to me
at the time, and to be honest, my mom couldn't cook,
and then hospital food, well, let's all admit that it's neither

nutritious nor delicious. We had a deal, see,
is the problem. And worse, there won't be any
negotiations until I break my end of the deal. Which
I refuse to do. See how he gets you? Soon as I do
that, he'll say something like, *Forsooth, and hear
ye, my son, whose faithlessness was veiled in
     conspiratorial venom, who
took of my fruit that which is reserved for angels,
and perniciously acted upon me, in spite of my name.*

Or something. Blah. And what do you say to that?
Talk about stacking the deck, and Christ, I've done
my best, but I'm hungry most the time. And hey,
I understand this is a pretty good deal compared
to most, but if you sign on the dotted line for a long
life, well that pretty much guarantee's you're not
gonna fucking starve to death. See what I mean?
And the nurses are no help either. I get two, maybe
three square meals a day (that I refuse to eat now), but
not one good piece of ass, or a decent bottle of wine, or
maybe even a nice compliment here or there. Is that
    asking too much?
I just figured that those would be included——a package
deal, if you follow me. Oh, and the electrical shock

therapy and the weekly cavity searches? What are those
all about? Listen, the thing is, there was a deal, (back before
he started to make everyone sign notarized contracts),
a deal shook on with my little weird hand right here,
    a gentleman's agreement
and by crock, when he finally takes me back,
I swear there's gonna be some hell to pay.

Crows Heart

——after Joshua Weiner

The west wind asks:
                    ——who would bury the blade?
And the dust mottled skin,

and the dirtied cracked nails
                              moan

one last color. And the tribal gait
bemoaning the stone
                              white man

river-hate
grasp the last Crow

by bruised wind pipe
and strike to hilt.

Crow's heartsblood brought close to Ute mouth,

the Crow's heart pressed tight to Ute lips.

Memphis

for Martin

The motel pool is shaded
in spots, black fading
into blue and grey
and the morning shine from
the sun is as mercurial
as it ever was, this last
sparkle of atoms firing
on atoms, just biology,
just simple first semester
junior college chemistry,
because water, salt, protein
and sugar make blood,
and it would be a good spring
day, he thinks, if it weren't for all
the sad sirens, or the vibrations
of bare feet on hollow concrete,
or the panicked shouting,
sounding at first like children
at play, and then like children at war,
and then feet shuffling in blood,
and the feet are like the feet he would
bathe, like the last actions of his
brethren, his good, dear friends,
showing their courage and love
in the storm of their footfalls.
Lord, they are heraldic angels
every one! Pray, keep them safe
lord, keep them under your grace,
for they usher in the new paradigm,
the day where the scales tip to balance.

They raise their arms in terrible ecstasy.
fingers pointing, pointing, to the window
across the street, where he cannot see
for the graying at the edges, but he prays that
the first light of the new heaven finally
shines down into the end of things.
Oh, the wet smell of concrete,
this last thing, a song of farewell,
like rain, as good and cool as any speech
he had ever seen or ever done.

It Makes Me Sad For Everyone

This raw knowledge that every poet must die
in the end, dashing themselves against rocks

sharpened by their own wit, crushed by semi's
filled with bananas, plums, tomatoes, the most

recent critical review. They are all heroes
to the end, diving into shark infested waters

just to see what it feels like to be bitten in half.
They spelunk their way into black caves, lighting

the way with wax candles, hang above infinite
chasms with frayed hemp rope, the jagged bottom

the last mystery, where guano and all that falls
gathers; and even when provisions fail, and ropes

break, they sing with the soulful knowledge that the poems
that light our way are always the poems that destroy us.

Notes

It is probably unusual, and likely inappropriate, to discuss intention and how it relates to failure in the process of building a successful manuscript, but I feel that it would be remiss of me to not address the varied and violent voices of soldier personas in the first chapter of this book. I suspect that for those who have read my first book, these voices might be confusing, so I offer this bit of clarification——while researching for the first section of this book, which was originally intended to be a manuscript devoted to elegiac poems about soldiers who return home to commit violence on themselves and others, I learned more than I would ever want to know about how we abandon our soldiers once we bring them home from the wars we wage. In the end, I learned that it would take me twenty careers, working without rest, to put even a tiny dent in the backlog of tragic stories generated only from the last two wars, let alone the uncountable number of them that exist since the first member of our violent species paid one person to throw rocks at another to defend their turf. That may sound like a harsh assessment. But it is all there in the record——we wage war, sing praise to our soldiers on their return, put them on floats in parades, and call it good. Then we fain surprise when they commit suicide, or kill someone close to them, or go on a killing spree like those already forgotten killers and victims in Fort Carson and Fort Hood. That said, I still owe them a book, or someone does. At the very least.

On a side note, there is also clear evidence that we are getting worse, not better, in dealing with post-war emotional problems: there is significant proof that the plays of Sophocles (who first coined "the thousand yard stare," and "shell-shocked," and was himself a general) were initially intended to be therapeutic, and ancient Greek theater's main purpose was to reintegrate warriors into a democratic society. It is clear to me that even our ancient ancestors had some sort of plan for their veterans, one that was inclusive and designed to bring them back to the fold.

Ultimately, the personas I took on were difficult in ways I did not expect. Not because I lacked the will or the stomach, but in the end because it would be a bit like devoting a career to the study of one brick from the foundation of a skyscraper. In the end, maybe I was not strong enough, or diligent enough, or prepared enough, to write that book (or perhaps, simply not the right veteran to write it in the first place), and for that I offer an apology, with gratitude, to all soldiers and their loved ones everywhere, because they all believe they are on the side of good and on the side of justice. And that is why I love them, and will continue to write for them. This book is for you.

Biography

Seth Brady Tucker's first book won the 2011 Elixir Press Editor's Poetry Prize (*Mormon Boy. 2012*), and was a finalist for the 2013 Colorado Book Award. He is a former Carol Houck Smith Scholar at Bread Loaf, and a Tennessee Williams Scholar at Sewanee, as well as the winner of the Bevel Summers Fiction Award from *Shenandoah*. His writing has appeared in various journals, most recently in the *Iowa Review. Chattahoochee Review. Poetry Northwest, Verse Daily. Indiana Review*, and *Pleiades*. He has graduate degrees from Northern Arizona University and Florida State University (PhD), and was a paratrooper with the Army's 82nd Airborne Division in another life. He is originally from Lander, Wyoming, and teaches at the Lighthouse Writers' Workshop in Denver and at the Colorado School of Mines in the Liberal Arts Department.

Photo by Rob Clement

Books from Gival Press-Poetry

12: Sonnets for the Zodiac by John Gosslee

Adama: Poème / Adama: Poem by Céline Zins with English translation by Peter Schulman

Bones Washed in Wine: Flint Shards from Sussex and Bliss by Jeff Mann

Box of Blue Horses by Lisa Graley

Camciones para una sola cuerda / Songs for a Single String by Jesús Gardea with English translation by Robert L. Giron

Dervish by Gerard Wozek

The Great Canopy by Paula Goldman

Grip by Yvette Neisser Moreno

Honey by Richard Carr

Let Orpheus Take Your Hand by George Klawitter

Metamorphosis of the Serpent God by Robert L. Giron

Museum of False Starts by Chip Livingston

On the Altar of Greece by Donna J. Gelagotis Lee

On the Tongue by Jeff Mann

The Nature Sonnets by Jill Williams

The Origin of the Milky Way by Barbara Louise Ungar

Poetic Voices Without Borders edited by Robert L. Giron

Poetic Voices Without Borders 2 edited by Robert L. Giron

Prosody in England and Elsewhere: A Comparative Approach by Leonardo Malcovati

Protection by Gregg Shapiro

Psaltery and Serpentines by Cecilia Martínez-Gil

Refugee by Vladimir Levchev

The Silent Art by Clifford Bernier

Songs for the Spirit by Robert L. Giron

Sweet to Burn by Beverly Burch

Tickets for a Closing Play by Janet I. Buck

Voyeur by Rich Murphy

We Deserve the Gods We Ask For by Seth Brady Tucker

Where a Poet Ought Not / Où c'qui faut pas by G. Tod Slone

For a complete list of Gival Press titles, visit: www.givalpress.com

Books available from Follett, your favorite bookstore, the Internet, or from Gival Press.

Gival Press, LLC
PO Box 3812
Arlington, VA 22203
givalpress@yahoo.com
703.351.0079

CPSIA information can be obtained
at www.ICGtesting.com
Printed in the USA
LVOW11s1313250417
532112LV00002B/110/P